The Sphere of Birds

Crab Orchard Series in Poetry
Open Competition Award

The Sphere of Birds

CIARAN BERRY

Crab Orchard Review

&

Southern Illinois University Press

Carbondale

Printed in the United States of America

18 17 16 15 5 4 3 2

The Crab Orchard Series in Poetry is a joint publishing venture of Southern Illinois University Press and *Crab Orchard Review*. This series has been made possible by the generous support of the Office of the President of Southern Illinois University and the Office of the Vice Chancellor for Academic Affairs and Provost at Southern Illinois University Carbondale.

Crab Orchard Series in Poetry Editor: Jon Tribble
Open Competition Award Judge for 2007: Cathy Song

Library of Congress Cataloging-in-Publication Data

Berry, Ciaran, 1971–
The sphere of birds / Ciaran Berry.
p. cm. — (Crab Orchard series in poetry) (Open competition award)
ISBN-13: 978-0-8093-2838-3 (alk. paper)
ISBN-10: 0-8093-2838-0 (alk. paper)
I. Title.

PS3602.E76365S64 2008
811'.6—dc22 2007026525

Printed on recycled paper. ♲

The paper used in this publication meets the minimum requirements of American National Standard for Information Sciences—Permanence of Paper for Printed Library Materials, ANSI Z39.48-1992. ♾

For Hope Vanderberg

I know the birds; would to God I was among them.

—*John James Audubon*

Contents

Acknowledgments

Many thanks to the editors of the following journals in which poems in this collection first appeared, sometimes in slightly different incarnations:

AGNI—"Trajectory"
Columbia—"The Sphere of Birds"
Crazyhorse—"Electrocuting an Elephant"
The Gettysburg Review—"Cold Pastoral"
Green Mountains Review—"Donegal Fences"
Low Rent—"Harbinger & Ghost" and "The Parsley Necklace"
The Missouri Review—"Topography with Storm Petrels & Arctic Tern," "A Beard of Bees," "Over By," and "The Act of Seeing"
Notre Dame Review—"Blindness" and "Foundlings"
Ontario Review—"Orchid," "Moving & Storage," "On the Anatomy of the Horse," and "Two Funerals"
Prairie Schooner—"Cuckoo Spit"
The Recorder—"April 1941"
The Southern Review—"Extraction"
The Threepenny Review—"For the Birds"
Turnrow—"Oblique Projection"

"Topography" was also included in *Best New Poets* 2006.

Many thanks to Jon Tribble and the Crab Orchard Series in Poetry, and to everyone at Southern Illinois University Press.

Thanks to the various astute readers and supporters whose sage advice helped shape this volume, including all my friends in the creative and expository writing programs at NYU.

Thanks especially to my family, to my fellow poets Ryan Black, Colin Cheney, Matt Donovan, Lorraine Doran, and Kathy Graber, and to my teachers and advisors Peter Fallon, Eamon Grennan, Melissa Hammerle, Stanley Kunitz, Phillis Levin, Philip Levine, and Cynthia Zarin.

Many thanks to Cathy Song for choosing this book and to the New York Times Foundation, whose support helped me write a large part of it.

Thanks most especially to Hope Vanderberg, for everything.

The Sphere of Birds

Cold Pastoral

A crow shot dead and hung from a steel pole
warns other crows away from a field of grain,
hard-won, where ochre ears change tack, go with
the wind. Its eye has been gouged out, sun beams
against the socket's black, turns into steam
the film of rain stalled there while, loose and swift,
breeze ruffles up the feathers, dries the stain,
the blood that's bloomed above the wound's neat hole.

Things weather fast here, soon bird will be bone,
brittle and white, dead twig snapped underfoot
where the sky alters in seconds, shine to shower,
and harsher truths hit home hour after hour—
the sundew snagging flies, settling to eat,
a fat gull's fractured keen that cuts through stone.

One

Orchid

I found one in the field behind my parents' house,
a single off-white bloom that stood erect
as though it meant to stab the sun in that late afternoon

in which I paused to let the dog piss on a stone,
then crouched to get a closer look at petal, leaf, stamen
of the flower Greek ancients believed sprang

from seed a mountain goat or escaped bull had spilled
as he withdrew from the warm loins of his mate.
Like the mandrake, which, they used to say, arose

from the last ejaculations of horse thieves and heretics
who dangled from the scaffold for their crimes
and fertilized the earth beneath their feet,

there was something dark about the flower there
among the sticky-lipped sundew that snacked on gnats
and the ragwort that ran rampant from a bog hole's black eye

to the weathered, gray fence posts that cut a crooked line
to the main road. A crimson stain on each petal
could have been taken as symbol for the blood spilled

by William Arnold or Benedict Roezl,
that irritable Czech with a steel hook for a left hand
who led troops of men with machetes and pack mules

out past their waists in alligator swamps
to look for fresh strains of a flower that grew high
in the limbs of pop ash and custard apple trees

in lands the words of missionaries had yet to penetrate.
And if not blood, then some other mark of shame
on a flower not native, but uprooted from the dirt

of the new world, bought out of pygmy graves
for jars of beads and packs of cigarettes,
shipped back to Dover and Portsmouth, roots cleaving

to yellowed femurs and skulls, sold with three taps
of the hammer to some inbred duke who loved
to give things names, to classify and order in an age

made strange, uncertain, by those upstarts Marx and Darwin.
Lady's Slipper, Coral Root, Late Spider, Early Spider,
Lapland Marsh, Heath Spotted, Bird's Nest, Bee:

even Darwin himself saw something in the flower
when he stooped to stare into the foot-deep nectar well
of a star-shaped bloom from Madagascar

and glimpsed in its deep, fleshy petal whorls
the direction of his own and our future,
finding a new meaning for the word adaptation

as he surmised there had to be a moth
with a tongue long enough to reach the bottom
of that purple font. *Orchid*, from the Greek

for testicle, flower more than flower, little enigma
that wrapped roots through the caked mud
of ages and kept hold, hard to believe its seed

(carried the way myth or truth is carried
on the breeze, or beneath the wings of birds)
ended up stamped into the dank loam of that field,

where it must have lain dormant for years
before opening out into the bloom
I plucked, took home, and stuck in a jam jar.

For the Birds

Something has pried open the body of this hare,
unpicked a seam from between the stilled hindlegs
to the middle of the slackened, gray belly.

Now the two sides of the wound part slowly,
like a mouth widening as it comes on the right word,
or that neat tear in the half-obscured lower thigh

at the center of the theater in Eakins's *The Gross Clinic*
where, as I remember it, the owl-eyed surgeon
seems so unmoved by the thick, scarlet globules

that glisten like cheap lipstick on his thumb
and the anguish a mother buries in her dress sleeve
as he explains precisely how he will poke

a scalpel into tendon, muscle, bone, to remove
the latest clot of gangrene from the left leg of her son
who might, if all goes well, last out the year.

Two assistants hold the patient down, while
a third and fourth, with their crude tools, keep open
the incision and stare deep into the mysteries

of the flesh, as eager for their time with the body
as the petrels, kittiwakes, black-headed gulls,
that tend the hare's remains up here in the near-

heaven of the dunes, all neck and beak and skirl
as they uncoil the intestines turn by turn,
divide liver from lung, pick out the heart,

squabble over the kidneys. Hauling away whatever
they can use, they rise through marram grass,
through shifts of sand, and disappear, leaving me here

to understand a little more what the dead mean
to the living, why every St. Stephen's Day
of that decade we lived on the outskirts of town

the same three freckled cousins, wearing straw hats
and masks, would bring to our front door
a single wren. One of them played a tin whistle,

his mud-scabbed fingers missing every third note,
another grinned as he held up their find in a jam jar,
while the third, his voice not yet broken, sang

a song about that king of birds "caught in the furze,"
that ball of roan and gray feathers punished because
its ancestor had once exposed the patron saint

of stone masons to those who pursued him
simply by singing from the wall the soon-to-be-martyr
had crouched behind. Like the saint, the bird

would suffer a harsh end—not stoned and left out
for the hooded crows, but stolen from its hiding place
deep in the undergrowth, fated to expire

behind that wall of glass, which must have seemed
invisible at first, when the boy's cupped hands
opened and the bird dropped down into its cage.

Half-starved as they stood there in old men's clothes,
those boys were also part of the cycle, and
would soon become their fathers so their fathers

could be earth, the oldest one driving a tractor back
and forth from the church, the one who sang
hanging dead rooks up in the fields to save the grain,

while the youngest boy, the one who held the bird,
inherited the title of village drunk and cleared
his mother's house of possessions to quench

a thirst that would land him face up in the ditch,
eyes glazed with a thin layer of ice, dead as the hare
struck down here in the dunes where, cold and prone,

the pistons of its legs proved no more than flesh
and bone, it lies empty as those blue tits Keats shot
to clear the air a few days after his brother

coughed up phlegm flecked with blood for the last time.
Keats, who was months away from his nightingale
and further still from Rome. Yet as he lowered the gun

to watch each ruffle of feathers fall to earth, he felt
sure the same blackness that had claimed poor Tom
was sprouting in his lungs and would blossom,

that his remains would mean no more than a dropped
apple to the worms the graveyard birds would yank out
of the earth and swallow whole, that he and each

of us would end up as coiled muscle in the wings
of house sparrows, a dull throb in the robin's fragile
heart, dissonance in the hoarse throat of a thrush.

Blindness

Whether arrived at in the womb or through old age,
or because hatred in a hoop skirt and whalebone corset
has been welcomed as honored guest into your home,

the result, it seemed, was much the same: a darkness
emphatic as when the clock's short arm breaks back
an hour to let the shadows loose over the lawn, to make

welcome the fall's first frost. In double science after lunch,
one boy argued it would happen if you touched yourself
too much or spent too long before the goggle box—

revenge of the body on itself by way of an unraveling
within the tissues, humors, rods and cones, so that
the soul's supposed door could no longer open to usher

in the objects of desire, to carry word and image upside
down into the flesh. Those fledgling years the sightless
were a nation unto themselves, their flag crow-black,

their head of state the shopkeeper whose eyes were like
two hardboiled eggs without the shells stirring below
the jars of clove rock and jawbreakers arranged in rows

across the shelves, whose identical twin was taciturn,
pure strange, forever, it appeared, *staring* into space.
They knew far more, I guessed, than we could know

about the grave, about the afterlife, and how the world
could be so cruel, why in the third act, the seventh scene,
of the play we were reading that year in school,

the King's daughter must conspire with her husband the Duke
who will use just his fingernails to gouge out the Earl's eyes,
leaving behind these two bloody sockets a loyal servant

will dress, as best he can, with "flax and whites of eggs."
Our teacher, whose vision was perfect, swore the walk
to Dover's chalk cliffs, its "crows and choughs," was metaphor

for something or other of how the future would describe
its arc, whispering softly into our ears, then leading us away.
Later, he told us of the cloistered monk who kept a poker

in the fire until it glowed a bright orange and he applied it
gently to both eyes, so that the dark he craved would be
seamless, so that he could not lose his way to what he saw.

Foundlings

1. "Wild" Peter

You come to us out of the woods, out of history's long corridor,
naked, mud-flecked but pure, wholly yourself, your yellowed teeth
bared in a crooked smile as you approach that lone haymaker's
stunned gaze. And what I want to say is turn back now, while

there's still time, while that man who's dropped his scythe and stands
completely still in that half-stubble field can put all this down
to the second beer his wife packed with his sandwiches, to some trick
of the light in the late afternoon, or of the mind after so many hours

alone. Go now before he reaches deep into the pockets of his coat
for the red apples he will hold—one in each palm—as, part pied piper
and part first sinner, he lures you towards Hameln. Foundling,
our world will dress you in a purple suit and make you the plaything

of kings, a curiosity who loves his gin and bites the heads from house
sparrows and wrens. Better to disappear again into the leaf-dark
you stepped from, into the rumor of your kin, said to stalk the pine
groves on all fours and suckle the pert teats of sleeping bears.

2. Victor

In Caucasus, whenever one of the sacred slaves wandered alone
into the woods, apparently inspired, the high priests had him
bound in golden chains and fattened on the best fruit and fowl
in the kingdom. After a year, a spear was driven through his side,

the future told by how the body fell. And so, tomorrow, the doctors
will come once more into your cell with their pencils and paper
to try to trace a line between instinct and learning, to probe
with questions in a language you neither speak nor understand.

In the meantime, you press your nose between the bars of the window
and welcome a familiar cold that tastes of loam and pine needles,
the sky low hanging, turning slowly pinker. Soon it will snow,
an unspoiled down will fall into the walled gardens of the Bicêtre,

obscuring the pathways and the outstretched palms of the statues,
swelling the waters of the pond you stare into sometimes, transfixed—
an unkempt Narcissus, unsure whose face it is that hovers on
that calm surface and why the hand he reaches up never meets yours.

3. Kaspar

That day you staggered like a drunk into the village square, you
carried your entire story with you. It was in that picture of a dead city
tucked into the red band round your hat, and in the rosary beads
and scribbled prayers that swelled your pants pockets—the loss

of place, the religious fervor of that vague figure you called *man,*
who came by sometimes to beat you, or to bring leftovers. You wore
so many scars, and, as you fell further into the glare, you must
have looked just like one of the mole people I've seen stepping

from tunnels, filthy and bruised, daylight searing the white balls
of their eyes, making them blink and cry up here where no one
welcomes them as seers. Not even the shoemaker, who stood before
his shop smoking a corncob pipe when you showed up without

the words to ask him where you were. Who could have guessed
that, years later, you'd find your way into his plosive tongue only
to plague us with the old questions: "Who made the trees?" you'd ask.
"Who puts out the stars?" "Where is my soul and can I look at it?"

Topography with Storm Petrels & Arctic Tern

On our first television set, a black & white,
the screen a square about the size of a trivet,
my brother and I watch Van Gelderen sketch
an arctic tern. First, the circle of the head,

its thick outline pointing towards the spiked
prong of the beak, which, all in one stroke, gives
to the sleek curves of a throat that veers
sharply towards the taut belly, then rises,

splits into the twin prongs of the tail.
And then the back, then the wings opening.
All of this happens at near double-speed,
the fingers furious in their markings

after the charcoal's brief hover above the page.
And now, his flits and feints having
shaded out the only eye that's visible,
that glut of dark feathers around the crown,

some sleight of hand or trick of editing
transmogrifies this stationary male
into a bird at wing above the outcroppings
and crags of *Inis Mór.* Holding its own

against the catch and drag of air, it looks
just like those two gray-brown storm petrels
in Audubon's watercolor—one of fifty
on display this week uptown. Already,

I've spent two afternoons wondering
if they're rival lovers or a mating pair,
one facing me, the other turned away,
their eyes fixed on each other in a gaze

that can only mean hatred or desire.
And what they seem to say, strung up just so,
hanging forever between heaves of gale,
is something about balance, about grace

faced with the great weight of the elements.
According to Edward Armstrong, we know
that during daylight birds use the sun to find
their way, and that at night they rely on the stars.

It's thought that they may orient themselves
using the earth's gravity, but the full mystery
of how birds navigate remains beyond our ken.
Enough then to admire whatever drives

the wings, that heart no bigger than the tip
of your middle finger, whatever name there is
for the instinct that keeps the tern facing
forward as it glides between hemispheres,

north to south and south to north again.
On his stalled crossing from Portsmouth,
Audubon could not paint those storm petrels
as they hovered just above a cursive wave.

Instead, he spent those wild days below deck
heaving the contents of his fraught stomach
into a laundry pail, trying hard to forget
it could be weeks before Liberty stuck her

arm out of the fog, the *Columbia* bobbing
like a pink buoy, its jolts and jars dousing
the flame in his paraffin lamp, stirring
whatever winged subject he carried home—

a tree pipit perhaps, or a chaffinch—to fix
its claws around the cage's bars and hold.
In a Carna we'll soon leave behind, so
that something small and feathered in us dies,

it is the year my brother and I find a jackdaw
with a broken wing, the year the fish farm
where our father works closes its doors. The tanks
in the hatchery are emptied of oysters,

the mussel rafts are dragged ashore, and most
of what we know vanishes like the wallet
and keys the magician picks from our old man's
pockets as he assists with a trick at the circus,

choosing a card, checking a bowler hat for holes.
Although all we know will never be returned.
Lying on his bunk, nothing left to empty
from his belly, Audubon stares through

an iced porthole at the almost black that runs
beyond the eye and thinks of how his life
will be a journey from one fixed point to another
with only open water in between, something

he ought to take no pleasure in, yet the knowledge
of it makes him almost happy. The chaffinch
is dying behind the bars and, in the morning,
will be tossed overboard without even a word.

And though Audubon will recover from this,
his latest bout of "the blue devils," he'll continue
to suffer the erosions of the body until he can
no longer lift a finger to enter the musculature of a bird,

until he can't even remember his own name.
And I'm sure he'd know exactly what I mean
when I explain that the future is a crew
of five or seven men in gray-brown overalls

who come to wrap the clocks and pictures
in blankets, to bear the couch and rocking chairs
out of that living room in which I sit
with my brother, eyes fixed on the screen,

hand hovering above a packet of crisps
as Van Gelderen's tern flies further and further
away, wings and body at first discernable,
then just a black dot, and then nothing.

Electrocuting an Elephant

Like mourners, or men setting out early for a duel,
they follow these six tons, this hunk of flesh,
muddy and whorled, this elephant they tried once to hang
because she'd killed three men and survived

their carrots laced with cyanide. Coney Island, 1903,
and the handheld camera that gets all of this down
is a clock for seeing, as Barthes tells us it ought to be,
the image forever ticking over as three men,

in sepia and near-silhouette, step through a vacant lot,
follow the lead of the burly handler, who carries
a sleek whip, a coil of rope, as he leads his charge towards
the spot where they will set two of her feet

in copper shoes. Think of the boy, who sat in front of you
that year in school, led by the ear to the corner
of the classroom because he couldn't spell vengeance
after three turns. Think of the bull, three summers old,

pulled by the horns towards the place of sacrifice
so that bees might rise up out of its pooled blood.
And this too must be the way they took Bartholomew
after he made the King's brother deny *his* gods—

one guard gripping the prisoner's left arm and the three others,
who follow, unable to muster a single word
as they march down the main street of their village
towards the blue edge of the Caspian Sea,

where they will dispose of this son of Tolomai,
taking turns to open him with knives. What do they think
as they skulk after the condemned, this trinity,
who are not quite men yet despite their pristine uniforms,

or these others like extras from one of the first westerns
with their hats and moustaches, their say-nothing expressions
that barely make it beyond the ground sand of the lens
and onto this reel that unravels as I find myself

thinking again about that boy who, in *Scoil Muire,*
sat in the front row of those battered desks
with the defunct inkwells, the dry hinges that opened
into a box to store your books? This time he's reeling off

the names of birds. He makes a fist and hammers it
against his skull to bring forth robin redbreast, stonechat, crow,
while the rest of us raise our hands with what we think
are the right answers and hold our breaths trying hard not to laugh.

The truth is, I can't remember his name, only the way
his clothes reeked of stale milk and hay, and how
his father once tied a frying pan between the legs of their mongrel
to discourage it from running after cars. I'd like

to whisper this story into the ear of the keeper
before the film goes any further, before they reach
the spot where a crowd waits, impatient,
shifting from foot to foot. I'd like to tell him how,

after those four boys have done their dirty work
and turned into something older than they were before,
Bartholomew becomes that figure above the altar
in the Sistine Chapel who holds up a tanner's knife

and his own skin, another saint made patron
to those who wield the tools that worked his exit
from this world. And though it changes nothing,
I want to explain how, when the elephant falls, she falls

like a cropped elm. First the shudder, then the toppling
as the surge ripples through each nerve and vein,
and she drops in silence and a fit of steam to lie there
prone, one eye opened that I wish I could close.

The Parsley Necklace

Before he gives himself up to the air that swirls and eddies
there just after dawn, Petit tests the steel wire with his toes,
makes that tensioned cable his own, a sort of extra limb
that will hold him more than a thousand feet above Church Street,

where the rush hour crowd, jackets over their arms, spill
from the subway scuffle. They are no bigger than a swarm of flies
from where the wire walker hangs his eye, feels for the fulcrum
in his balancing pole, and then, with a sharp intake of breath,

takes his first step, trusts where he must go. All of this happens
thirty years ago, when I'm just four, a nervous middle child
who takes sick on every car journey of more than five miles,
retches and heaves until there's nothing left but yellow bile.

My mother's tried a series of folk-cures—a length of chain
suspended from the rusted tow bar to spark all the static
out of the car, a parsley necklace fixed around my throat,
where it serves as a sort of vegetable amulet, but nothing works.

Something about the body's wish to move at its own pace,
resistance to the confined space of our beige Renault 4,
another fear to add to a list that includes German shepherds,
earwigs, heights. I never leave the house without a pocketful

of plastic bags. On his high wire, Petit moves with the grace
of a gymnast, his walk is pure dream work, a sort of being
and, at the same time, not being within the confines of his
skinny frame, this conclusion to what began with a toothache,

in a Paris dentist's waiting room: on a table there the magazine
in which he found a sketch of the new towers and traced a line
between those roofs to make the distance smaller, more bridgeable.
Spreading the photos now over my desk, I wonder what Hart Crane

would make of this, the Brooklyn Bridge suspended somewhere
over Petit's shoulder as he steps towards the center of the wire
and genuflects to acknowledge the crowd he knows will have
gathered below with their briefcases and half-smoked cigarettes,

each head tilted back, each mouth and pair of eyes opened into
the same stunned look of those who sat on deck the morning
Crane appeared, still drunk and unshaven, one eye blackened
from his brawl with the cabin boy he wanted only to love,

mournful as he draped his coat over the railings and, wearing
just his pajamas, plunged into the gulf, where his body became
so much sand and foam. In this moment, where everything
is pure present, and these black & whites are something I can

almost step into, it is Crane's shade that hovers a few feet
above Petit in the shape of the all-seeing gull that catches
the tightrope walker's eye as he lays out on the wire, defying
all the bones in his body, right leg crooked for balance, left leg

dangling free, only those few inches between him and an almighty fall.
Or else the gull is death personified, arrived to stare our hero
out, hoping soon to knock him off kilter and bear him away
into the whatever. Although Petit only stares back and smiles,

then rises, steps towards the other side, where a young cop waits,
amazed, with one hand on his gun. On long journeys, smoke
of my father's pipe billowing, the parsley necklace dying
round my throat, I'd stare out the window and count telephone

poles, trying to make the journey go quicker, trying to trick
my body towards false calm. I'd keep a total in increments
of ten, lose my place and start over. It was another way
for me to learn about the beginning, the end, the in between.

Two

Harbinger & Ghost

> I live with a strange sense of revelation
> and never know what the day will bring
> —*W. B. Yeats*

That bottle of aquamarine glass a Clare witch
used to scry. The pool of ink where a professor
from Trinity claimed he'd seen spirits move.
The abstract was always reached through the concrete,

and perhaps this was the real lesson the poet
meant to learn watching the goblet glide the ouiji board,
taking his tea with fussy mediums, or entering
the residence of one David Wilson, a deranged

chemist and part-time solicitor. "A kind of earhole
into the unknown" was how he described his invention,
this box filled with a length of pipe and a brass
drum, something his guest would later christen

the metallic homunculus. All afternoon, it picked
out the cards that Yeats had marked in red,
then popped and clicked with coded messages
from Leo Africanus, Oscar Wilde. And, for a while,

it seemed as if they'd bridged the great gulf
between room and room, the rubber tube
Wilson attached and held up to his ear, like the receiver
of a telephone, for once no interference on the line,

the first voice to press full sentences towards
the listeners telling of a great crush on the other side.
As if it fits, as if it's connected, tonight, staring
down from the overpass towards the L.I.E., I thought

the stalled cars looked like rows of souls lined up
in purgatory, their headlights, two and two and two,
stretching back through the dark further than I could see,
were torches carried by the lost Sister Catherine

made us pray for—heads in our hands, knees
grazing off the hardwood pews, St. Anthony looking down
on us from his plaster of Paris statue in a past,
which is both harbinger and ghost, where we were

more than just bodies, silenced before the altar,
or split into three groups bright afternoons to march
around the playground, arms by our sides, the nun
tapping her stick off the concrete *deas, clé; deas, clé.*

Sometimes, after a day of rain, I think "angels"
because of how the light fractures and spreads to wings
on the drenched road, the glimmer soaring
as the traffic shrugs forward, turning the blackness

a fool's gold that's just enough to split the winter trees.
And who could blame Yeats for what he set out
to know that morning in St. Leonards-on-Sea, or for what
his wife fished for later—not casting her line

from a window in the tower and waiting for a rainbow
trout to take her bloody worm, but settled there
at the kitchen table, a pencil loose between her first
and third fingers, as she waits for the dead to enter her.

Over By

Swell pummels rock, darkens sand, creeps upshore
        to stir beach stones and periwinkle shells,
        the bone-dry bladderwrack and sea lettuce
out of which swarms of flies rise, disturbed,
to hang their scrim above the waterline,
        a low fog of wing, thorax, abdomen.
        The give and take of waves, their push and drag,
symbol for all that is given and snatched away,
or so the old story goes, the fish wife's tale
        in which we're born and die on the tide's turn,

shucked out into the world when water's high
        against quayside, barge, and quarterdeck,
        then loosed from this, the body's current stilled
when the sea retreats, folds in upon itself,
leaving behind odd boots, smoothed shards of glass,
        each new day's array of carcasses:
        an unwanted dog drowned in a black bin bag,
an eyeless pollack, a black-headed gull,
sometimes a fisherman, or a humpback whale.
        All that's pelagic, all that's nautical,

must end up on this wind-battered shore,
        hence all those sea fables and their metaphors,
        all that blarney about Oisin and Bran,
the latter convinced by homesick Nechtan
to leave behind their island of women
        and sail back to a mainland where everyone
        they'd known had gone to ground, become the soil
they had once tilled and hoed. And so, come to the end
of his own voyage, returned centuries on,
        and unaware of how he'd cheated death,

Nechtan extends a foot from the currach
        and, on touching home turf, is turned to sand,
        a small urn's worth of ground down flesh and bone,
a splash of bright atoms the squall will catch
and disperse over beach, bog, glen, mountain,
        minute fragments in the great beating down
        to topsoil, humus, loam that is endless.
Almost bent double with his crooked spine
as he stood at the end of the gravel path
        leaning hard on a hawthorn walking stick,

Micí Dubh Thimí used to enthrall me
        with wild stories of his time *over by*—
        which meant anywhere across the water,
anywhere that could be reached by boat,
hence the harsh Edinburgh or Glasgow
        Micí and his brother had once sailed for
        to carry hod or work shovel and pick,
but also, perhaps, where he thought it would end
after that gravel path met the main road,
        after the final waters showed their course

towards, let's say, an outcrop of white rock,
        the sea unkinked and sun-dappled below
        an island full of whiskey and tobacco,
where he would settle with a Woodbine and a glass,
full, perhaps, of the same bliss as this cormorant
        above my head that, lured by the shimmer
        of rockfish, gathers its wings and plunges
like something dropped, reckless with instinct.
A pure thing, without doubt, without question,
        as its beak breaks the water's cold surface

the entire bird is swallowed up, consumed
by spume and backwash, slap and sway of brine.
The Bilqula ancients believed the soul
would quit the body like this, in a winged shape,
breaking from the nape of the neck, rising
into whatever sphere it would enter.
To others, it was a fine dust, essence
that could escape through the navel or nose,
the mouth, the feet, by way of a fresh cut,
a yawn, a sneeze. Or else it was a thumb-

sized manikin who sat on a plush throne
in the crown of the head, who resembled
in every aspect the form of his or her
carrier; who, when the body slept, was prone
to wander, dropping down through the ear;
who, when death came, would permanently leave,
begin that slow journey across the sea,
through blanket bog and field, or venturing down
that beaten track poor Orpheus followed
to plead for the return of his child bride,

her ankles still swollen from the snakebite.
I love these old stories, each conjecture
like a stone skimmed across the blue surface—
although (I know) stones sink, although
even the rough ones are worked smooth
and pushed against the dunes by the spring tides,
and, then in winter, carried to sea again
to be worked over, smoothed stone to pebble,
and pebble to this sand I step across
picking up scallop shells, a mermaid's purse,

dragging this grief that's endless and useless,
        that resolves nothing and consoles nothing.
        The light now giving way, a beam of white
from the lighthouse on a nearby island
scans the rough bay for any sign of life
        and finds a trawler motoring towards the line
        where the sky becomes sea and vice versa.
A reef bell cries among the orange buoys,
and now, reaching its height for the last time,
        that cormorant tucks in its wings, and dives.

A Beard of Bees

In a scorched July field near Stinson Beach,
        I watched a man in a white polyester suit
                remove the queen from her wax and amber cell
deep in the hive. He handled her casually,

        as though she were a chess piece—the carved
                ivory symbol of herself, and not the gnarl
of pheromones that controlled her golden horde
        in their flights among the asters and lupines.

                Gently, stroking her soft back with his thumb,
he placed her in the cage beneath his chin,
        tucking her in before he closed the little hatch
                and stepped backwards, twelve or thirteen paces,

his boots hoof-tapping off the dry, cracked earth
        until he stopped and the whole afternoon
                went still. Silenced, those of us gathered saw
the five o'clock sun make long his shadow

        over the parched oat grass, the wire fence
                that held, at every barb, knots of goat hair,
the odd magpie or mockingbird feather.
        We waited, observers among the bees,

                our being there reduced to ears and eyes
when the swarm came, at first as a faint drone,
        the turning over of a small engine, then as
                a loose thread spooling from the hive,

the bees unraveling, forming a line
that covered so quickly the short distance
between the honeycombs and their trapped queen.
They dipped and landed on the keeper's cheeks,

settled into the beard he wore, mouth almost shut,
nostrils blocked with cotton wool. And it struck me
that all of this must be to do with death:
the way the bees had scrieved across the air,

their see-through wings thrashing in unison;
the keeper's need to feel against his flesh
that knot of tangled muscle and barbed sting;
our need to watch, awestruck, like the rough crowd

at a hanging, as the moment cracked open,
the field and the minutes suddenly rent,
unfixed. We know the queen emasculates
the drone during mating, ripping the phallus

from his abdomen so that he bleeds to death
within the hour, but what about the beard of bees,
that thick black mass like a burned out heart,
alive with malice and ardor, some feral need?

Donegal Fences

A weave of corrugated iron strips, upended
pallets, and car doors various shades of discolor
cover the gap that's rusted or been broken

through the wire fence that separates this last
fertile acre from a bog marked only here and there
by tractor paths and half-starved, black-faced

sheep that seek grazing. Almost washed
from a byre's crumbling gable, bold, uneven
capitals recall the boy who found "orgasm"

between the covers of his mother's *Woman's Weekly*
and slipped out late under the moon to scrawl
his new word to the first surface he came on,

releasing it, as he had to, despite the priest
he served Sundays on the altar, and his own father,
who would, when he discovered, uncoil

his famous leather belt and let its buckle
work scarlet welts from the young artist's back
and thighs. Strange, isn't it, how the bump

or bruise rises out of the flesh, as though it
had been there all the time, just waiting
for the blow to make it known? Either he slung

a rope around that solitary oak, threaded
his thick neck through and jumped to his revenge,
or that boy's taken a boat and train towards

the scaffolds of Camden and Bethnal Green,
where he carries a bucket or a bag of trowels
after whichever of his brothers, cousins, friends,

are building up and tearing England down.
Not half-a-mile from here, behind the boarded
snooker hall that sits below what was once

the boxing club, and what is now a store
for shop-soiled mattresses, they found last year
five or six syringes, the needles blunt, the tubes

viscous where a group of boys, too broke
or bored to simply drink and fumble at their girls
on the green baize, had been getting out of it

for weeks on the same three-liter flagon of cider,
fists clenched until a vein exposed its crooked line
and, one by one, they punctured their pale arms

to sail above the rooftops of four bars, three
chip shops, a post office, into the luscious name
of some place they could never reach by thumb,

a New Orleans or Amsterdam of the mind's eye.
In the absence of what we crave we improvise,
make do. Take my brother-in-law, a stonemason

and landscaper who made, for my sister's last
birthday, a glasshouse out of nothing but the odd
windows and scraps of wood he'd gathered

from the gardens where he spends each rain-free
hour. This summer, in their backyard a few
townlands away, those cracked panes harbor

tomatoes, green peppers, delphiniums, each one
a symbol for the recovered, a small sign
of hope that will last, perhaps, until the fall's

first frost. Or take, in the far corner of this field,
the rusted bath that serves as water trough
for a piebald heifer and last month's still-skinny calf,

although I like to think the landowner or,
better still, his soft-spoken daughter, might come
down here sometimes out of pure boredom

in nothing but a robe she drops around swollen
ankles before testing the surface with her toes,
then stepping in to soak under the stars and forget

everything. There's something to the way
the old men round here put it, their grammar still
inflected with the Irish, so that the words

often hit on a separate truth. For them, it's not
today, but *the* day, as in "it's a grand day the day,"
as if there's only one to be got through.

Cuckoo Spit

Mulkerrins was older, always on the cod,
swearing to God that bats drank blood from cows,
that dog piss could cure warts. Behind his house,
amongst the sedge and ferns, the sally rods
his mother kept to tan his hide, there stood
a drystone shed where that year's spuds were stored.
Inside, Kerr's Pinks fingered their white shoots towards
the light that skulked beneath the door. We would
steal in there when the coast was clear to look
through his Uncle Colm's stash of dirty books.
Mulkerrins would name the parts, "fanny" and "dick,"
and, once, undid his pants to do a trick
of hand movements and moans that made him split
and bleed something pure white, like cuckoo spit.

Oblique Projection

The chalk squeaks like a frightened mouse
between the drawing teacher's frail fingers and thumb
as, for the fifth week in a row, he drags lines

of forty five degrees from the four corners
of a rectangle, out into the blank space
of the board, where they hang for a moment,

fragments suspended, until he pulls down verticals
and slots the horizontals into place,
making his fractured shape a solid whole.

At twelve, we pity no one but ourselves,
we think the old man's crazy as his stick-short-
of-a-bundle son, who takes the yellow bus

that stops in every town round here
to pick up those with their eyes and limbs askew,
those who wear helmets to protect themselves.

As he writes the name of the lesson
between parallel lines and explains once more
how to add depth to height and width

we make peashooters out of hollowed pens
and pass around a crumpled centerfold
that shows two smiling blonde women, naked

and shaved between the legs. Two months from here
the boy who sits alone in the front row
will fall between the sandbags we've dropped

as stepping stones across the surface of a slurry pit,
and sink down to his waist, his mouth,
his eyes, and finally his hair, which will float

for a moment like a discarded wig before
he disappears. Twelve years from here, one
of those red-haired twins will take the other's eye

clean out with a beer glass sharpened over
an oak bar in the same month our school chaplain
welcomes the bishop, who will come to town

with his gold crosier, in his best emerald robe,
to confer holy orders onto the slumped
shoulders of that boy with the acne and the bottle-

thick glasses, who passes on the photograph
without even a glimpse. For the rest of us, though,
nothing much will stir. We'll inherit

our father's wellingtons, their Massey Fergusons,
and fade into the gray of our school uniforms,
the gray that has consumed this confused man

who stands between us and the expanse of the board,
delivering almost line for line and word for word
the same lesson he taught last week and the week before,

while we wait with our soft black pencils, our plain
white sheets, our homemade weapons and pornography,
about to copy down what he has drawn.

The Sphere of Birds

Pigeon-gray sky, dulled brick, skeletal trees, everything
        moving towards elegy this season of lost light
and sudden gusts in which the pages from a *Village Voice*

        fly south, and a small army of house sparrows
advances across this bench, hoping to share what's left
        of my sandwich. Famished, haggard, a little desperate,

they halt a foot from me and tilt their heads, peer up
        through eyes earth-brown, prehistoric (a throwback
to the archaeopteryx), and wait until a boy, running,

        drags a stick through the railings, scattering them
into the sphere of birds—the airy realm that, in one of my favorite
        films, the quiet hero fashions a rise into. At least

ten times I've watched him, Icarus in jeans, launch from
        the handlebars of his best friend's bicycle
to float on homemade, paper wings above the refuse sacks,

        burst mattresses, the dogs and rats of the local
landfill. And perhaps what he knows there among the crows,
        the girlish squeals and funeral skirls of gulls—

that sense of airiness, of erasure—is what my brother knew
        all those years ago as he sat almost entirely still
at the kitchen window, embracing whatever came to the feeder,

        eye three inches from his sheet of butcher paper
as he daubed the washed-out reds of a male stonechat's breast,
        or described the arc of a yellowhammer's wing,

immersed in line, stroke, and color until the swallow
of the rain in the downspout and the dampness
in his chest that meant another day from school were overcome.

)

Why do they bother, what is it both boys want except
the soul sprung from the locked box of the self,
one doing his best to scale the ladder of the air,

the other rapt up in the workings of his wrist,
and both of them reminding me of the Caladrius, that all-white bird
said to symbolize Christ, a more literal taking away

of sins, as it drew the symptoms of any non-fatal human illness
with its stare and carried them into the sun to burn.
Later in life, my brother will collect bones: skull of a curlew,

the ribcage of a herring gull, a convex structure
like a currach's wood frame, large enough to hold a robin or
a wren. Later, the boy, who takes off in the film,

will come back with shellshock from a lost war, will squat
and hop locked up in a white room where a chair
and a cast iron bed is all the furniture. But before he reaches

that blind corner, that cruel bend, there is still time
to flap his arms, to kick at nothing, until the current gives
and he falls screaming towards a stagnant pool

banked on all sides by slashed tires, defunct washing machines,
the detritus of Philly in the Fifties. Before this,
there are those loose myths that persist around our blue house

halfway up that Carna hill. If the magpie builds
her nest high in the sycamores there will be no storms all summer.
If the swallow flies too low there will be rain.

And, who knows, one of those Ridge brothers—three
bachelors who live around the hill a little bit
and seem to us older than bog or brae—might still tell you

that the barnacle goose is not a wild fowl
but a fish with wings, born of the sea's chaffing against scraps
of driftwood or the silent hulls of passing ships.

)

According to the book I've been reading, the archaeopteryx
was a dun creature roughly the size of a crow.
It croaked and squawked and groaned and climbed the trees

on hooks and claws attached to its clipped wings.
It could flap and leap and partially take off but never fly—
not unlike these house sparrows of mine, migrants

that no longer go south for winter, non-natives brought here
to keep the insects down, or to remind some
sentimental immigrant of home, they settle once more

around my feet, peer up at me, impatient for crumbs.
If, as the author of my book claims later, the size of a bird's heart
is as important as the flight muscles that allow it

to become "active in the air," then the heart of the archaeopteryx
must have been small, fearful, as, sometimes,
I think my own heart is small—robin or wren trapped in its cage

of bones, like the lovebirds our Aunt used to keep
above the stove. "Ernie" and "Bert" our cousins called them, although
one was a girl, which didn't matter when the cat

from next door strayed in, drawn by the shrill notes of their song.
She snuffed them out without even a touch,
her green eyes fixed against the cage's bars enough

to make those little hearts implode. And so,
we dug a hole in the garden and buried each of them in a jam jar.
Sometimes I think that everything is its own elegy:

the Latinate grandeur of archaeopteryx, all those myths
on the Caladrius, the tossed boxes of bird seed
and cuttlefish, the cat's meow, and here, on this "hilly island,"

the way we leave our names on bars and funeral homes,
and disappear towards suburb, prairie, grave. The letters
peel now from Mahon & Sons, a neon light flickers

and dies above the Liffey Bar as it awaits the wrecking ball
of the future. Planes swish and drone above
the blanket cloud, hulls full of passengers like homing birds.

)

Somewhere towards the middle of the film there is that scene
in which the boy's beloved canary flies back
through a window that's been closed, while his best friend,

in uniform, walks away from everything he knows.
All those viewings and still I'm not sure if it means something
about change, its vicious speed, or about wings,

their pure fragility. Something on how death's an opportunist,
        light on her feet, and forever seeking out an opened
door? Or perhaps a much more general shattering . . . My brother

        went so far into painting that he could no longer
bear to raise a brush. What he came up against inside himself
        was glass, those green eyes settled at the cage's bars.

In one of the last pictures he produced, a boy's shaved skull—
        his own, I think, although it could be anyone's—
bends forward in supplication and regret, floats huge

        above the charcoal pews and gothic arches of a church.
And though I set him back at the window, and fill
        his pallet and horsehair brush with watercolor blues

and greens, though I press rewind and watch the bird rise
        from the shattering to fly backwards out of the reformed
pane, it's not the same, it's nothing I could ever want.

The Hive

Put your ears against the warped slats of the hive
        and the walls hum, just as they did that night
                I woke up to find the house alive with moans,
my two roommates having come home with men

        and, through the walls, now wrestling love from them,
                something bright and beautiful in their drunken abandon,
in what was forgotten as they tangled, limb
        and limb, all queen and drone until first light arrived

                and the milkman carried three bottles up the steps.
In Virgil's world, there was nothing like this:
        "they neither delight in bodily union, nor melt
                away in the languor of love," he wrote of his swarm,

his bees born of a bullock's blood after the sacrifice
        and, later, picked from leaves, gathered whole
                into their parents' mouths and carried home,
or so the poet claimed, mistaking need for such

        small miracles, the apiary a world without desire—
                something to want and fear, to want and fear,
like the butterfly tattoo on the back of the first girl
        I ever saw completely nude apart from glossy photographs,

                brief snippets of film. I know now it was a swallowtail
she'd had etched over the notches of her spine
        as though it were rising clean out of her backside,
                suggesting we carry something colorful and winged

in the folds of our intestines, and not our own
version of soil, harbinger of the earth we'll lie under.
All that summer of her, I hunkered in the dirt
and bent towards clumps of squat, green plants,

lifting their leaves to see if any fruit lurked underneath,
ripened and red, ready to be plucked, the sun above
Sussex tearing the skin from my back, layer
after layer, as I made my way from runner to runner.

It was my first time alone in a country I'd been
warned was very different from my own.
At night I got drunk on cheap vodka and puked up
strawberries. I was learning about freedom and restraint.

"Tear off the wings of the kings: while they linger
not one creature will dare set out on its airy way,"
Virgil reveals later, confusing his genders,
yet describing perfectly his golden mean for bees

as he watches a battalion of workers glide
from cassia to lime blossom, or whatever
the gods have set in bloom. I think the heart must
be like this, a sort of hive sending its workers out

from flower to flower, leading the drones into the snow
every winter, always doing a dance to please someone.
It has its swarm, its sting, and, if you rub a finger gently
round its rim, it starts to hum, as though flexing its wings.

Three

Trajectory

Three months before we moved here
　　　the avenue collapsed, the asphalt
　　　　　　splitting neatly down the seams

of the white lines, boulder, gravel
　　　and strut that had buoyed up the outer
　　　　　　layer crumbling into the weed-choked

lot below, bearing away a house
　　　that had stood vacant there for years
　　　　　　the way a flood might carry off a cow.

And although no one was on the road
　　　that hour to feel the ground give way
　　　　　　beneath their brake and clutch, although

workmen have begun to reconstruct,
　　　slotting wood beams into girders
　　　　　　secured to the bedrock, mounting

a wall they're sure will hold, I can't
　　　help thinking of the road revoked,
　　　　　　its black rug dragged from under us

so that there's nothing left to do
　　　but fall—as, sometimes, on the edge
　　　　　　of sleep, I'll feel myself topple

from roof, staircase, step ladder, or
　　　no surface at all, and tumble slowly,
　　　　　　achingly, not towards bare sidewalk

or tiled floor but back into my own
crumpled body, its tangle of tendon,
muscle, bone. Exit and entrance, entrance

and exit: these were the concepts
we played with fifteen years ago
after a school performance of *Faustus*,

two boys standing front to back
outside the library, one joining
his hands below the other's ribs

and squeezing hard until the breath
oozed from his partner and we stepped in
to guide that limp body to ground,

where it looked so calm, peaceful,
until a spark flickered and then caught
in those dimmed eyes as our friend

stuttered back into himself to tell us
about darkness, about stars, the sheer
bliss of his winged emptiness. Today

I gazed for hours at photographs
from a village in northern Kazakhstan
where odds and ends from rocket ships

keep falling, sometimes a wing tip,
sometimes an entire booster engine.
One picture frames a sheep farmer

and his wife—their faces wind-burned,
deep with crooked lines—holding up
the toboggan and crude snow shovel

they've fashioned from the latest fall.
        Another shows six sorrel and white
                heifers laid out in the luscious grass

where they seem to embody ease
        until you realize they're not asleep
                but dead, killed outright by the part

that fell to them suddenly from
        a cumulus sky. You never know
                what might happen, we say, and yet

we know exactly, though not when,
        the body's trajectory always down-
                wards: hoof, udder, and gut flush with

the same longing as the skimmed stone,
        the building that totters on the fault line,
                or the green globe of that overripe apple,

real or imagined, in a Woolsthorpe
        garden, that allowed the young Newton
                to reach down "from hence to the center

of the earth" and explain, by way
        of four theorems and seven problems,
                our attraction to all that's beneath us.

Moving & Storage

Heft of a vanity, a chest of drawers, box springs
and mattresses, clocks and mirrors padded with blankets,
sofas and loveseats, each standing lamp, and, once,

the Steinway Baby Grand Jed and I lowered
from a fourth floor balcony in the Castro, our sneaker soles
squeaking off smooth cement as we tried to split

the weight into fair shares. This was my punishment
for leaving home so finally at the third try. I'd put
a distance of ten thousand miles between myself

and that damp island only to turn up broke at Harrington's
to ask an ex-cop and ex-serviceman from Kinvara
if he would take me on, though I could do little more

than spit and smoke. The rope burned through
my newly hardened palms as I gripped and loosed
on Jed's command, letting the piano jerk down

towards our boss, who stood in a blue blazer,
both hands raised, opening, closing, like a small bird's wings
while he screamed "lower the fucker, take the strain."

Later, in Blondie's Bar in the Mission, he would
crack himself up again telling the waitress we were two
of his illegitimate sons or, broody with whiskey,

would cock his thumb and barrel his forefinger,
pressing the nail into the smooth nape of Jed's neck
to illustrate how the Nazis had disposed

of those his battalion unearthed outside Dachau.
Solemn, he would describe the almost grassless center
of a field, clank of his shovel's lip against a stone,

a soldier next to him stooped to retrieve a pair
of smashed glasses while another came on the first scrap
of cloth, the stench of rotting flesh growing

stronger, blood in the soil, then all that remained
of an entire village, limp bodies piled up
like sacks of grain. "I came here with nothing,"

he would say, "just two worn pairs of pants and an address,"
as he nodded once to order the next round
or fumbled with the keys to the Deluxe Cadillac

he'd drive half-scuttered back to Half Moon Bay,
where his wife was dying in their summer home
as a tumor the size of a tangerine ripened in the left lobe

of her brain. "Lower the fucker, take the strain,"
he barked, as our heads bulged with blood and our backs
stretched, arms still raised as, weeks later,

in his store of scuffed armoires and stained lounge chairs,
he'd raise them once more to play conductor
to the quiet Polish boy with the glass eye,

who could not afford to buy "at any price," but
came in anyway sometimes to pry Rachmaninov and Liszt
from the hollow of that string and bone machine,

which should have dragged us cleanly from the roof
and crushed the man standing helpless beneath
its mass of tautened wood and wire, and battered ivory.

April 1941

In a Belfast of smokestacks and linen mills,
as a crane in the shipyard creaks to a stop
above the lough and men in work clothes spill

through the dock gates, my grandfather walks home
past girls who spin loose skipping ropes and jump
while their brothers thump a leather ball

against a gable end. Dusk seeps into the red
brick streets the experts say Hitler will never bomb.
A boy hawking *The Newsletter* cries "Delia

Murphy for the Ulster Hall" and my granda
passes down the Falls just as a quarter moon
appears above the new munitions plant.

On reaching his front door he stops to note
how the blackout order is defied by house lights
all across the city's west. Inside, he takes

his son Patrick onto his knee and greets
a wife who labors at sideboard and stove
to make enough of rationed beef and potatoes

for four children and a forever famished husband.
Her plump belly brushes the cooker knobs,
as, within the watery globe of her red womb,

my mother, perhaps nineteen inches long,
points her wee head towards the open, makes
ready to be born into this mid-war month.

But before she tumbles out into this world,
two hundred Heinkels and Junkers must swarm
across the Irish Sea, their shadows black crosses

on calm water, their cranked engines all hum
and splutter above the cormorants and guillemots
that dive for mackerel. Beneath the weight

of shells, the York Street spinning mill must
split and spill six stories of timber, concrete
and steel into bedrooms and living rooms on Vere

and Sussex Street. Delia Murphy must try
to sing "Three Lovely Lassies" above the drone
of air raid sirens, while fifty miles away,

at Glenshane Pass, fire crews who've paused
to let their engines cool, watch the flames billow
above North Belfast. My grandmother's waters

will break over the kitchen tiles as volunteers
empty the Falls Road Baths and fill the deep end
with the unclaimed dead. My mother's head

will come bloodied between her mother's legs
as an exodus of cars and cattle trucks rattles
away from this city where, just now, all is calm.

Three hours before the first bomb whistles down,
my granda takes his place at the table, prepares
a pipe, while his wife arranges cutlery and delft.

The Act of Seeing

The optometrist tapes a patch over my left eye
and asks me to read off the rows of capitals
he projects onto the white wall opposite. I can make out

only blurred bellies and dismembered stems,
fragments that represent nothing except themselves
or the first crude letters a child might scrawl

between parallel lines as he negotiates the alphabet.
Between slides, there's an empty square of light
onto which I could throw shapes with my fingers—

long-necked giraffe, a dog with floppy ears,
or one of those rabbits my brother and I found
on that stretch of no-man's-land above the beach,

where two hundred of them scurried to and fro,
unable to find the way back to their holes. For months
now, I've been joining dots round everything

that's more than a few feet away, adding eyes and ears
to blank faces, letters to subtitles and street signs,
redrawing the lines that fall short of my retinas

and seeing mostly what was never there,
like those creatures beyond the beach that seemed
so unlikely, so out of place, even before

we captured one and held it up into the light
and stared at the thick layer of white that obscured
its opened eyes, silenced and only then realizing

that all of the rabbits were blind and terrified,
that winter would see the beach littered with bones.
And maybe there as well we saw, just a smidgen,

into the world to come, saw something
of what Samuel Johnson knew, almost sightless,
and muttering violently under his breath

as he added a third definition of pain to his lexicon,
writing "sensation of uneasiness" from Bacon,
then putting aside his empty quill until the spasms

subsided, the shaking quelled. It takes the doctor
only five minutes to confirm I need glasses
and have needed them for at least ten years. Now

he adjusts the chair and lays me down and drops
a thick, yellow liquid onto the surface of my eyes,
dilating my pupils to five times their normal size,

so that my irises almost disappear, leaving just
these two black holes into which he stares,
through a lens the length of a shot glass, to read

what's written on my retinas. How strange and intimate
to be seen into like this, the back of my eye flashing
onto his as he scans its mother-of-pearl surface

for any sign of change, the act of seeing reduced
to its viscous minutiae: conjunctiva, cornea, and lens,
the same layers thirty of us cut through in the soft,

bloody bulls' eyes our teacher brought back
from the abattoir so we could see, for ourselves,
the bright clusters of rods and cones, and the severed

optic nerve that had, just a few hours ago, borne
images of grain, grass, mate, and water trough
into the damp whorls of the creature's brain. That day

we learned that sight was not a miracle, but
a funneling of light into the flesh through the same portals
now pried open in me that allow another man

to see inside until, satisfied that everything's in place,
he sends me out into an afternoon that's become distant,
smudged, a blur of gray buildings and passing cars

through which I carry just this crumpled note
of instructions for the lens crafter, who'll shape metal and glass,
set a neat frame round all that's before me.

On the Anatomy of the Horse

In this picture, the skin of a jennet has been peeled back
so that we can enter a beneath in which the ribs are a series
of staves balancing the cairn stones of bones with names
like atlas and axis, precarious digits of the neck, beyond which

the blood vessels of the head are a network of rivers and rivulets
feeding the flared nostrils of the damp nose, the weather-weary
look of the right eye. And perhaps there's that same look in the eye
of the old master as he buries a knife into the spent flesh of a mare

to watch the muscles open like blood flowers, to examine the joints
from flank to foot, knowing that, to capture the essence of anything,
you must cut into its heart, peel back the layers, enter—although
the horse beneath his hands is horse now only in name, become

the maggot-fodder of after, mere dimensions he will note,
try to reciprocate to mould a steed on which to place a statue
of the duke's father. And I imagine Leonardo thinks of God
as he runs his thumbs over an exposed vein or measures the liver

with his fingers, just as he thought of God entering the corpses
of thieves and rapists to paint saints, burrowing for something
that might explain laughter or ecstasy, the joy of the cavalryman
as he hurtles across the battlefield, leaning hard into the withers

of a mount that carries him towards death. Watching this fighter
rise from his saddle and point his spear, I remember the badger
my father skinned, cutting away the cracked drum of the heart,
casting it downriver with the snapped strings of the sinews,

the bagpipes of the lungs that say the body's just an instrument
the wind plays out of tune, leaving only this scraped pelt I run
a hand over, pressing stained fingers to my lips to taste of musk
and spoor, to know, somehow, that the room in which I stand

will collapse under its own weight of stone and thatch, that
the wild ponies, which appear sometimes near dawn to graze
the strip of grass that runs along the middle of our lane, will thin
out until the last of their number is corralled into a cattle truck

and borne away, for everything we know must disappear. Dusk
entering his dusty studio, the corpse beginning to fester, I imagine
Leonardo dousing his hands in a bucket of water to wash away
the blood, that, later, he will forget to eat, too busy wondering

how to make the dead thing look alive, thinking of the holiness
at work in the living. Leafing through the sketches in his mind,
he'll picture a bronze stallion kicking its forelegs through midair,
or balanced on the shattered ribs of an expired soldier, when,

out of nowhere, there appears the almost collapsed shape
of the draft horse that dragged the plague dead through
the back streets of Florence, head bowed to the prompting
of its master's reins and a chain-smoker's wheeze to its breathing.

Extraction

Up on the X-ray screen, my teeth shimmer and smoke,
a clutch of milky ghosts diffusing through a film of black,
their dug-in roots exposed down to the jaw's bedrock

as Doctor Turner talks about John Keats dying in Rome.
He thinks the odes are the best poems ever written
and I'm not going to argue. That nerve, the one that's causing

all the pain, sits "right there," he explains, trapped
between the bone and errant tooth, his finger poised below
what looks like a botched knot or the faint outline

of a worm, something foreign, something that doesn't belong.
"In the spring of 1819 a nightingale had built her nest
near my house," writes Brown. He tells us that Keats felt

"a tranquil and continual joy" in the bird's song
before going on to explain how, one morning, the poet
placed a chair beneath the boughs of the plum tree,

and sat there for two or three hours, lost in the layers
of his own being and in the knowing of the singing,
writing his way through and beyond the pain, his mind

swept clean, reaching neither for fact nor for reason.
All this week, as if to ease my own aching, I've been looking
at pictures of extractions made without anesthetic:

Der Zahnbrecher's "The Toothdrawer," Gerrit Dou's
"L'Arracheur de dents," and a photograph by no one known
from what looks like Russia or the Ukraine around the turn

of the last century. Here two men in black suits,
with close-cropped hair, bend towards the opened mouth
of another who, in his fear, has kicked over a chair

and braced one foot against an upturned leg. To keep
the scene as still as possible, the assistant has wedged
his boot into the patient's thigh and grips both his hands,

tugging the arms sideways to stop the struggling. I can see
a vague smile starting from the corner of his eye
as the tooth puller wiggles his wrist to tear the bloody thing

out in one go. And I wonder who or what the patient
curses now, if it's just these two opportunist toughs
who drive a knackered horse and cart from town to town

and, in backrooms, lay out their filthy tools, charging
only a few rubles to cure your pain through pain. I wonder
if he curses God or his own body, that crude shape

in which the ache has found a home, that vessel
he must carry back alone to a cold and empty house,
an unmade bed. And I remember a knee pressed

to my chest at age fourteen, how the dentist talked
wrestling and football scores as he pinned me
to the squeaky leather chair and demanded that I open

wide, wider. The beam of light he shone into my mouth
was so bright it seemed almost holy, like something
from a TV documentary about near-death experiences

in which a poor soul describes their ascension
from the slackened body into a pure white, where a favorite uncle
or a long-lost wife called out from beyond the blaze,

welcoming them into the afterlife. And as the forceps
tightened round my tooth, I wished for such a light
to gather me into a realm where there was no need

for Novocaine, or for this man's form to hover over mine,
hand in my mouth until that pre-molar broke free
of the numbed bone, leaving just this hole, an ache

that would thaw slowly, and the short walk back
to the waiting room. In late November, 1820, Keats writes
to Brown from Rome "I am so weak (in mind) that I

cannot bear the sight of any handwriting of a friend
I love so much as I do you. Yet I ride the little horse."
Yet I ride the little horse, and who doesn't? Later,

in the same letter, he says "for it runs in my head
we shall all die young." And sure enough, three months on
he's gone into the earth, the ether, into the fraught

words of his poems and letters, the scraps of lines
that circle the head of Doctor Turner as, two days after
the X-ray, he watches his assistant fix the mask

over my mouth, while he stands back and waits
to pull this tooth that is a sign of growth, of my supposed
wisdom, although, like everything, it's arrived late.

"As though of hemlock I had drunk, or emptied some
dull opiate to the drains," I can feel the gas slowing down
my heart-rate. I'm thirty one, and I'm about to go under.

Two Funerals

1. Emily Dickinson

They raise you up onto their hard shoulders, your beloved Irish gardeners,
each with a set of rosary beads in his pockets, their leader, Tom Kelley,
fighting off tears, his right hand square against a box that's cross-heavy,
the left arm of his Sunday suit empty, just as it is in the only photograph

of him that exists in which he sits between his wife and her sister,
and reminds me a bit of Abe Lincoln, hair slicked to one side, beard
trimmed
unevenly. Eyes blinking to adjust to the glare, they raise and carry you
from the gold bier, one muttering a *Hail Mary* under his breath,

another halfway through an *Our Father,* while a neighbor, twisting the
handlebars
of his moustache, wonders at your choice of pallbearers—these refugees
from potato blight and war, one missing teeth, another an amputee, one
wearing boots because he has no shoes. And yet, with so much dignity,

they carry you, laid out on the casket's inner shelf, a will-o-the-wisp figure
in a white dress, your face the same old bent sixpence, though more serene,
your body freed of its electricity, dead as the dark matter of nail and hair
that will continue to sprout months on from here. All this, and nothing else

as far as I can see, however much I'd like to say that you've simply slipped
along the path between the trees, become the mare that gnaws through
her tether and wanders to wherever the good grass is. There are the
buttercups,
there are the bees that lift their pot bellies from flower to flower, although

their buzzing is not really a requiem, as a friend will claim later in a letter.
There are these six sunburned laborers who carry their Miss Emily through
the hay barn and past the clay beds, where your marigolds bloom early
this year, pausing below the ledge from which you used to lower gingerbread

to the local school children, the star turn in your own fairytale, which has
now reached its close. In a whisper of *Glory Bes,* the procession moves onto
Triangle Street, up ahead, opened in earth, the hole in which they'll place
the skin and bones it comes down to because we cannot fully enter metaphor.

2. Leonardo Da Vinci

"Consider first the end," you wrote once, from right to left, though you
were only thinking of painting, and not the body opened and entered
without incision, and whatever the essence that made it stir removed,
leaving only the heft of what remains to be carried by these six taciturn

chaplains, brought in at your request, though they know little or nothing
of the deceased. Loose vestments swishing over the silent lanes, they
lead the way for three curates and a bulbous prior, around his head
a dim halo of flies that will follow the cortege to the chapel on the hill,

where your earthly vessel will be laid out to await a burial at which sixty
near-beggars will carry tapers in your name. Their palms will burn
as they try to shield their flames, while, outside, the bored gravedigger
leans over his spade, picks the dirt out of his nails, scratches his balls.

For him, it's work, he couldn't give a shit who's the latest to step beyond
the red-chalk boundaries of the flesh into that cave you describe, somewhere
in your notebooks, stooping before—one hand clamped over your knee
for balance, the other peaked across your brow to keep the sun at bay

as you lean from side to side, trying hard to see if there's anything
in there. Where does the force that stirs the hand backwards and forwards
across the page go when the heart stops stammering and no air enters
the chambers of the lungs? So many times I've asked myself this question,

waiting, in shuttered rooms, for my turn to stand before a neighbor's coffin,
to gaze at the veined lids drawn down over the eyes, the skin so pale
it's almost translucent. I can say only that, three centuries after the first
fistful of earth falls back into your grave, your bones will be raised again

into this light, this air, where a finch will build her nest in your ribcage,
concerned with nothing but how rain brings out the worms, while two local
urchins, skipping school, kick your skull round like a pig's bladder,
laughing as if one of them had just revealed the punch line to the perfect joke.

Notes

"Orchid": William Arnold and Benedict Roezl were nineteenth-century orchid hunters. The incident involving Charles Darwin is recorded in his *On the Various Contrivances by Which British and Foreign Orchids are Fertilized by Insects*.

"For the Birds": For the story of John Keats shooting blue tits, I'm indebted to Andrew Motion's biography *Keats*.

"Blindness": The play referred to here is Shakespeare's *King Lear*. The quotes in the poem are from act 3, scene 7, line 105 and act 4, scene 6, line 14.

"Foundlings": This poem relies on various accounts of these three so-called feral children. The type of ritual sacrifice mentioned in the second part of the poem is described by James Frazier in *The New Golden Bough*.

"Topography with Storm Petrels & Arctic Tern": Gerrit Van Gelderen was a Dutch naturalist, artist, and filmmaker whose work used to often appear on Irish television. *Inis Mór* is one of the Aran Islands. The phrase "the blue devils" is taken from John James Audubon's journals. I'm grateful to Shirley Streshinksy (*Audubon*) for her account of Audubon's transatlantic journeys. Edward A. Armstrong's book is *The Life and Lore of the Bird*.

"Electrocuting an Elephant": The film referred to here is the Edison Company's *Electrocuting an Elephant,* which features footage of the execution of Topsy the elephant at Coney Island. The idea from Roland Barthes is taken from *Camera Lucida*. The name Bartholomew means son of Tolomai. *Scoil Muire* is Irish for School of Mary.

"The Parsley Necklace": For his description of the walk between the World Trade Center towers, I'm indebted to Philippe Petit *(To Reach the Clouds).*

"Harbinger & Ghost": The epigraph is taken from Yeats's letter to Lady Gregory dated January 4, 1918. *Deas, clé* is Irish for right, left. L.I.E. is an abbreviation of Long Island Expressway.

"Over By": Several passages in this poem refer to the medieval Irish text *The Voyage of Bran (Imram Brain),* translation by Kuno Meyer. The Bilqula people's belief in the flight of the soul is outlined in Frazier's *The New Golden Bough*. A "currach" is a small rowboat.

"Oblique Projection": This poem is for Bryan Boyle.

"The Sphere of Birds": The film referred to several times here is Alan Parker's *Birdy*. The book mentioned is, once more, Edward A. Armstrong's *The Life and Lore of the Bird*. *Hilly Island* is a translation of the Algonquin *Manna-hata* (Manhattan). This poem is for Ewan Berry.

"The Hive": The quotes in this poem are from Virgil's Fourth Georgic, translation by J. W. MacKail (1934). The second quote has been altered slightly.

"Trajectory": The quote here is from Isaac Newton's letter to Edmund Halley dated June 20, 1686. The photographs mentioned are by Jonas Bendiksen.

"April 1941": I'm indebted to Jonathan Bardon *(A History of Ulster)* for his account of the Belfast blitz.

"The Act of Seeing": The disease referred to here is myxomatosis.

"On the Anatomy of the Horse": For his description of the artist's attempt to build a bronze statue in memory of Duke Francesco, the father of Ludovico Sforza, I'm grateful to Serge Bramly *(Leonardo).*

"Extraction": The letter from Keats to Brown is dated November 30, 1820. The lines quoted near the end of the poem are from Keats's "Ode to a Nightingale."

"Two Funerals": I'm indebted to Richard B. Sewell *(The Life of Emily Dickinson)* and Serge Bramly *(Leonardo)* for their accounts of the events surrounding their respective subjects' funerals. I am also indebted to Eamon Grennan whose talk on Dickinson helped inspire the first part of the poem.

Other Books in the Crab Orchard Series in Poetry

Muse
Susan Aizenberg

Lizzie Borden in Love: Poems in Women's Voices
Julianna Baggott

This Country of Mothers
Julianna Baggott

White Summer
Joelle Biele

In Search of the Great Dead
Richard Cecil

Twenty First Century Blues
Richard Cecil

Circle
Victoria Chang

Consolation Miracle
Chad Davidson

Furious Lullaby
Oliver de la Paz

Names above Houses
Oliver de la Paz

The Star-Spangled Banner
Denise Duhamel

Beautiful Trouble
Amy Fleury

Soluble Fish
Mary Jo Firth Gillett

Pelican Tracks
Elton Glaser

Winter Amnesties
Elton Glaser

Always Danger
David Hernandez

Red Clay Suite
Honorée Fanonne Jeffers

Fabulae
Joy Katz

Train to Agra
Vandana Khanna

If No Moon
Moira Linehan

For Dust Thou Art
Timothy Liu

Strange Valentine
A. Loudermilk

Dark Alphabet
Jennifer Maier

American Flamingo
Greg Pape

Crossroads and Unholy Water
Marilene Phipps

Birthmark
Jon Pineda

Year of the Snake
Lee Ann Roripaugh

Misery Prefigured
J. Allyn Rosser

Roam
Susan B. A. Somers-Willett

Becoming Ebony
Patricia Jabbeh Wesley

A Murmuration of Starlings
Jake Adam York